30 Days to Better Financial Awareness

To Sis Dawkins —

May God always bless you with health & wealth!

Helen Crawley-Austin

Helen Crawley-Austin

Copyright © 2015 by Helen Crawley-Austin.

Mastering Money: 30 Days to Better Financial Awareness

By: Helen Crawley-Austin

Printed in the United States

ISBN: 978-1508700616

All rights reserved solely by the author under international Copyright Law. Except where designated, the author certifies that all contents are original and do not infringe upon the legal rights of any other person or work. No part of this book may be reproduced in any form without the expressed written permission of the publisher. The views expressed in this book are not necessarily those of the publisher.

Scripture quotations are taken from the New King James Version®. Copyright © 1982 by Thomas Nelson Inc. Used by permission. All rights reserved. Scripture quotations taken from the Amplified® Bible, Copyright © 1954, 1958, 1962, 1964, 1965, 1987 by The Lockman Foundation. Used by permission." (www.Lockman.org). Scripture quotations marked NIV are taken from the Holy Bible, New International Version,® NIV. Copyright © 1973, 1978, 1984 by Biblica Inc.™

Cover Design by The Q Train

FOREWORD

For as long as I've known Helen—and that would be my entire life—she has been a student of mastering money. It all started when we were kids, and she received a treasure chest savings bank for Christmas. Whenever she got extra money from allowances, straight-A report cards, or our grandparents at Christmas, she saved it in her little treasure chest. While my brother and I chose to spend our extra money on immediate gratification like candy and toys, Helen chose to sacrifice and save for a greater purpose. We watched her treasure chest grow from pennies to dollars, from dollars to hundreds! What a powerful lesson she taught us about living with less to save for a rainy day.

Whenever we played Monopoly, she was always the banker. While the rest of us held on to our money because we were overwhelmed by fines and rent, she invested in properties like Boardwalk and Park Place, eventually buying entire blocks, all utilities, and the railroads. As she collected rent from us, she would use that money to purchase more assets until she created an entire monopoly. At the end of the game, after she had taken every single dollar from us, including my parents' money, she would teach us that our idea of holding on and trying to save our money wasn't enough; we had to multiply it by investing and creating multiple streams of income so that we could become the lender and not the borrower, like her! Although it was just a game, right before our very eyes, it became a simple formula that we would witness her play out in life as she matured.

Helen left home and mastered whatever she took on, whether it was earning an advanced degree in engineering, rising in the ranks of corporate America, starting a successful real estate company, or launching a program that would teach thousands of people how to master money. She worked hard at it all until she mastered her craft.

Mastering Money is a program Helen developed more than twenty years ago. It is both spiritual and practical in its makeup and delivery. Through her workshops, people learn the concepts of money management and how to apply them to their finances. More importantly, they begin to change the way they view money, themselves, and their relationship with money, which enables them to commit to the practice and hard work that comes with mastering money. In short, Mastering Money was born out of Helen's passion for helping others handle money God's way and live a financially healthy life as a result. Today, I am living debt free and recently purchased my new home with cash, avoiding $95,000 of interest rate payments to the bank. She has certainly helped me make wiser investments, and I know she can help you. That's why she's written this incredibly important book.

Sylvia Crawley
WNBA Coach
CEO of Coach Plus Inc.
Owner of Monarch Magazine
www.coachplusconsulting.com
www.monarchmagazinc.com

INTRODUCTION

MASTER YOUR MONEY OR IT WILL MASTER YOU! I'm excited to help you start thinking about money differently through the reflections in this 30-day devotional guide. In these pages, I share my reflections on Mastering Money using biblical principles and quotes from people who have influenced my life over the last several years. My goal is to raise your awareness about the societal, psychological, and spiritual influences of financial wellness.

I became a student of financial wellness some years ago, and I have been meticulously taking notes from teachers, speakers, ministers, friends, and authors who have made profound statements, teaching series, and/or sermons. My prayer is that this little book will provide you with support to overcome financial challenges you may have had for years.

Mastering Money: 30 Days to Better Financial Awareness is a microcosm of my workshop, which I conduct at churches and conferences throughout the country. So you don't have to wait for Mastering Money to arrive at a church in a city near you. You can begin learning the steps and principles of the program now. The book is an introduction to sound money practices such as budgeting, debt elimination, saving, investing, and giving. It doesn't ask you to add to your head knowledge, as much it calls for you to meditate on those financial principles until they become embedded in your heart and ingrained in your philosophy. For example, the world teaches us that there's good debt and bad debt. Mastering Money teaches us what Scripture teaches us: There is no such thing as good debt. And that's one of the best things about this book—it goes straight to the source for complete truth to back up every principle it asks us to meditate on.

The Bible has a lot to say about money—more than 800 Scriptures in all—and there's a reason for that. Scripture teaches about the importance of saving, lending, budgeting, paying debt, and investing—again, all topics you will meditate on while reading this book. What you do with money, or how you handle it, matters a whole lot. Money management impacts every area of your life. It can mark the difference between life and death, that is the abundant life Christ came to give everyone (imagine the freedom of living debt free) and the loss people often experience when they don't manage money God's way: broken relationships, enslavement to creditors, property loss, and so on.

What you'll find in *Mastering Money* are rich insights on the principles of money management inspired by quotes from some of my heroes of faith and endorsed by God's Word, along with a little homework. Each day includes an action step to help you begin the process of seeing money differently in order to begin managing it differently. Realizing the money you have truly belongs to God is the first step to learning how to master money. So this book considers stewardship from a broader perspective.

What's truly impactful about this financial devotional, and why it's critical you meditate on each entry and complete every action step, is it emphasizes the importance of managing all of your resources—not just your money but also your time, your talent, and so on. It provides a great sense of hope that you can overcome any financial disaster or setback when you make a conscience decision to handle money God's way. If you tend to avoid the topic, perhaps because you're afraid to see just how deep in debt you are or you think there's no hope for your situation, this devotional is for you. *Mastering Money* is going to revolutionize how you think about money and what you do with money. If you view money properly, you will handle it properly.

Becoming financially healthy and attaining wealth is a bit like becoming an elite athlete. It doesn't happen overnight, but it takes practice, hard work, and sacrifice. Does that mean you won't make any mistakes? Of course not, but you don't stop trying, you don't stop practicing, after you do. As you read this book, be sure to follow through with each action step. Remember that practice makes perfect—so don't take one play off.

You were not created to live within the financial limits of our society. Each of us has the ability and power to break strongholds in our lives. And financial bondage is a stronghold that must be broken. I firmly believe God gives us the ability to do just that—break the patterns and cycle of debt and financial bondage and be free.

Now, I'm not going to be talking about anything new. My goal is to shed new light on what you know, feel, and may be experiencing. I want to start by telling each of you that you can be financially healthy. Financially healthy means spending less money than you make and having the ability to pay all of your obligations on time, put some in savings, and give some away! You will have to change your thinking, your habits, and—in some cases—your friends, but believe me: once you make up your mind about being financially healthy, nothing can stop you!

The truth of the matter is getting your finances in order might be one of the greatest accomplishments in your life. I believe that once you harness the discipline required to manage your finances, you will have established the habits to tackle many other challenges you experience in life.

Why is the battle over finances such a big ordeal? Here's why: our commercial society has managed to make us believe that we need stuff (in some cases, too much stuff!) in order to be happy. You know the mantra: We just have to have that expensive car, the big house, and the designer outfits! After all, the script goes, "We work hard every day at our 9 to 5s, so we deserve some happiness regardless as to how long it takes us to pay it off—as long as we can afford the monthly payment." Sounds familiar, doesn't it?

This is the case for most Americans. How do I know that? I know that because American consumers have racked up $11 trillion in consumer debt. High credit card balances, mortgage debt, and student loans are causing families to carry a heavy load. Happiness for some has a big, fat price tag on it. Based on an analysis of Federal Reserve statistics and other government data, here is the U.S. household consumer debt profile as of November 2014:

- Average credit card debt: $15,611
- Average mortgage debt: $152,192
- Average student loan debt: $32,264

In total, American consumers owe:

- $11.74 trillion in debt (an increase of 3.3% from last year)
- $882.6 billion in credit card debt
- $8.14 trillion in mortgages
- $1.13 trillion in student loans (an increase of 8% from last year)[1]

As you read this devotional guide, take time to reflect on each principle, especially as it relates to your relationship with money. Be determined to implement changes in your financial life. I'm committed to assisting you on your journey. Jump into my debt-free revolution at www.helencrawleyaustin.com.

Once you have finished the book, I hope you are driven by your need *and* your desire to fix what's broken with your finances and change your financial outlook for the better—and for good. Are you tired of being the servant to money? Are you ready to master it? Then don't hesitate another second. Begin your journey toward financial freedom—now go to practice.

DAY 1

A journey of a thousand miles must begin with a single step.
—Lao Tzu

Lao Tzo was an ancient Chinese philosopher and poet. His words have been used to inspire many people to overcome life's challenges. They are a most fitting start to this book due to the opposition most people face when making the decision to get their finances in order. Although many financial experts recommend starting with a budget, I disagree. Understanding and defining your "why" is the first step to financial liberation. Your personal "why" defines your ultimate purpose for gaining financial independence. Until a person experiences the pain caused by financial disarray, he or she never will be able to exercise the discipline required for total debt elimination or to save enough money to prepare for anything significant.

I recommend spending at least thirty minutes in a quiet place to nail down your heartfelt reason for getting your finances in order. It should contain specific details, including the names of individuals you want to assist, places you want to visit, and organizations to which you want to donate. In order to clearly direct your attention, focus, and passion, your "why" should draw out your emotions. I would contend that it should be tear jerking. Your "why" is what you should think about to keep you motivated and on track until you reach your goal.

Your journey toward financial health may not take a thousand miles, but it does require that you take the first step. I encourage you to take that first step today.

In the Word...
Then the LORD answered me and said:
"Write the vision and make it plain on tablets, that he may run who reads it."
Habakkuk 2:2

ACTION STEP

Write down your personal "why." Be specific. Add as many details as possible, and then add a date to your "why" to turn it into a goal.

DAY 2

It takes as much energy to wish as it does to plan.
—Eleanor Roosevelt

I love Eleanor's quotes because I've spent many wasted hours wishing I could be out of debt with millions of dollars in the bank, only to realize that wishing got me nowhere. I bet you just "wish" you could be out of debt. Wouldn't it be wonderful if everything we wished for came true? Unfortunately, that is not how life works. Instead, you have to plan to get what you want. With money, you have to plan where you want to spend it. As I said in the introduction of this book, you have to master your money or it will master you.

In money management terms, the second step to getting out of debt is establishing a budget, or what I like to call a spending plan. Don't get overwhelmed by the need for a spending plan, for it involves simply listing all your sources of income and all of your expenses. Hopefully, your income is more than your expenses, and the money you have left is your disposable income. The goal is to increase your disposable income. You may have to cut your expenses, start a business, get a raise, or unfortunately get a second job. In most cases, determining creative ways to cut expenses is sufficient for most people.

Whatever you need to create your spending plan is your navigator for the necessary actions you need to take for your household.

In the Word...
The plans of the diligent lead surely to plenty,
but those of everyone who is hasty, surely to poverty.
Proverbs 21:5

ACTION STEP

Commit to completing your budget by the end of this week. Get all your bills and/or bank statements and list out all your expenses. You may have to estimate your grocery bill and miscellaneous expenses. The key is to get it down on paper or in a spreadsheet right away. Be sure to track what you actually spend as you progress through the month. You may be surprised by your spending patterns. Feel free to go to the Mastering Money website—www.helencrawleyaustin.com—to get our budget template.

DAY 3

I have learned over the years that when one's mind is made up, fear diminishes.
–Rosa Parks

Rosa Parks was an activist in the Civil Rights Movement. In my opinion, Rosa Parks is the best example of a person whose determination to move past the possible fear of death not only changed her destiny but also the destiny of thousands of others who still benefit decades later from her act of courage. It takes courage to step up to the plate and tackle personal finances.

For many, personal financial management is unfamiliar territory. Not many of us were taught about finances in high school, college, or even church. (I have a master's degree and can't recall one class on personal finance during my years in higher education!) Consequently, many people are afraid of honestly facing their finances. They spend without a budget. They become overwhelmed with past due bills and then are afraid to answer the phone for fear of facing a bill collector. Fear paralyzes. Fear keeps us stuck, yet there comes a time when each of us realizes it's time for a change. It's then when we must make up our minds to move past fears toward change.

Make up your mind once and for all to move past the fear in order to do what's required to get your finances under your control. Like Rosa Parks, let nothing and no one hinder you from improving your future! Once you begin Mastering Money, you will have peace of mind and much more hope for your future.

In the Word...
For God has not given us a spirit of fear, but of power and of love
and of a sound mind.
2 Timothy 1:7

ACTION STEP

What fear do you have to face and overcome before you can move forward in Mastering Money? Take a few minutes to pray about any fears you have about money. Make up your mind to face them. Write them down so you can come back a year from now to celebrate your accomplishment of moving past them. Like Rosa Parks, you may be the catalyst to helping others in the future. Think of the financial impact you will have!

_____

_____

_____

_____

_____

_____

_____

_____

_____

_____

_____

_____

_____

_____

DAY 4

Courageous acts contain both wisdom and justice, coupled with the characteristics of patience and experience.
–Bishop Arthur M. Brazier

While discussing Mastering Money with me one day in his office, my former pastor Bishop Arthur M. Brazier of Apostolic Church of God in Chicago, Illinois, shared with me some of the challenges he faced running The Woodlawn Organization and the courage required to fight social and financial injustices in the 1960s. He described the courage and the strength required for African Americans to save for and purchase a home back then.

I believe the balance between when to spend and when to save requires wisdom and patience. The balance between when to spend and when to give requires wisdom, justice, and experience. In any case, courage is the foundation required for all four. On the surface, you wouldn't think it takes courage to spend, but I beg to differ. It takes tremendous courage to sign your name on paperwork indicating that if you don't make the monthly payment on time, your interest rate will jump from 7.99 to 21.99 percent.

Let's use that same courage to exhibit the discipline required to find extra money to save for investments. Let's exhibit the courage and wisdom needed to drive a used car that you can pay cash for versus a $30,000 car that looks nice but eliminates the extra dollars you could invest in your child's college fund. Let's flip the switch! Don't stop thinking about today; just consider the impact your decisions will have on your future, then have the courage to make the hard decision to exercise wisdom.

In the Word...
I can do all things through Christ who strengthens me.
Philippians 4:13

ACTION STEP

In what ways are you willing to exhibit courage in your finances? Are you willing to have the courage to drive a used car for which you can pay cash (temporarily, of course)? Or are you willing to give up your smartphone for a basic phone to save on the additional cost? I challenge you to combine courage and wisdom in your finances to increase your savings for a specific goal (e.g., retirement, college fund, or vacation). List three sacrifices you can make that would require courage on your part.

DAY 5

It is time to be a conqueror!
–Dr. Charles Stanley

I know we talked about courage on Day 4, but given the importance of the courage required to change the course of your finances, I think it is worthy of another day.

Joshua is my favorite Old Testament biblical character. Dr. Charles Stanley, the famous television evangelist and senior pastor of Atlanta's First Baptist Church, refers to God's development of Joshua's courage in the quote above. The book of Joshua starts out describing Joshua's transition into leadership as he took over as the leader of the children of Israel after the death of Moses, the former leader. God continued to remind Joshua to be courageous because he knew Joshua would want to know that He was with him as He was with Moses. This was a monumental assignment for Joshua; that's why God kept telling him to be strong and of good courage.

Conquering anything takes courage. Courage is the quality of mind or spirit that enables a person to face difficulty, danger, pain, etc., without fear. Dr. Stanley pointed out that God knew the battle of Jericho was coming, and He knew what would be required of Joshua. God told him not to turn to the left or to the right. Why? Because you can't go by what seems right, and Jericho did not seem right. It takes courage to go to a new destination as a new leader with instructions that seem impossible. Financial independence may be a new destination for you, and you may be new at developing a spending plan, but muster up the courage like Joshua and conquer your Jericho!

In the Word...
Only be strong and very courageous, that you may observe to do according to all the law which Moses My servant commanded you; do not turn from it to the right hand or to the left, that you may prosper wherever you go.
Joshua 1:8

ACTION STEP

What area in your life do you need to conquer? Take a courageous step. List the areas that have blocked you from managing your budget and wealth so you can conquer them. Meditate on the Word of God so you can make your way prosperous!

_____

_____
_____
_____
_____
_____
_____
_____
_____
_____
_____
_____
_____
_____
_____

DAY 6

God can bring greatness out of a mess!
−Joel Olsteen

Like Pastor Charles Stanley, Joel Olsteen is a popular televangelist and senior pastor of a large church. He oversees Houston's Lakewood Church. I admire his approach to delivering his messages because they involve simple, everyday tasks and thoughts that help you digest a profound truth. During the delivery of this quote, he mentioned how grocery stores put damaged products on the damaged goods shelves at a discounted price. The question is, why are they still selling them if they are damaged?

Here's why: Many damaged canned goods are still good as long as the dent or damage does not create even a pinhole-size opening. As the former owner of a food safety consulting firm, I would advise against purchasing damaged products because of the potential of botulism; however, I did get his point. The products are labeled damaged goods, but if you open the can, normally the contents on the inside are perfectly good.

You may have made a mess of your finances, but the good news is it is never too late to clean them up. You can develop the discipline required to make the most of what you already have. Stop feeling damaged or diminished and beating yourself over past mistakes. Admit the areas in which you mismanaged your finances and commit to spending less than what you make. Save what you have left over and be determined to have life abundantly.

In the Word...
The thief does not come except to steal, and to kill, and to destroy.
I have come that they may have life, and that they may have it more abundantly.
John 10:10

ACTION STEP

The first step to changing direction is to admit that you have a problem. Confess or admit to God that you have not effectively managed the resources that He gave you stewardship over. Commit to pray over this area of your life. Write down three things you can do to ensure you are spending less than you make each month.

_____

_____

_____

_____

_____

_____

_____

_____

_____

_____

_____

_____

_____

_____

DAY 7

You cannot take every penny that comes your way and spend it!
–Andrew Wommack

For years, I avoided watching televangelist Andrew Wommack. He always sat at a desk just talking into the camera without a podium or an audience. How boring, right? One day I just happened to be watching his broadcast—and oh my goodness! I couldn't believe it! His message truly blessed my heart. I grabbed my iPad as I do every time I hear a good word and *voila*, here I am writing about him.

Andrew Wommack was teaching on stewardship and plainly stated, "You just cannot take every penny that comes your way and spend it. There will be ups and downs, but you simply must think about your future. Don't get caught up in the incentives." I agree with him.

I remember after getting my first job in my twenties, all my friends were buying new cars. I drove a used car for which I paid about $3000, or $130 per month. I drove it until it rusted out. I still think I should have just got it painted. Who knows—I might still be driving it today. Anyway, while everyone was spending their money on expensive clothes, shoes, and cars, I was buying real estate, paying my tithes, and giving to others. I'm not insinuating that others were not giving, but I know they were not buying investment properties.

The moral of the story is, I too could have spent every penny on stuff, but I was focused on my future. I have to say, although having investment properties is not as easy as people think, it is by far one of the best things I ever could have done early in my life. It not only brought me financial gain but also taught me valuable lessons I would not have learned anywhere else.

In the Word...
And likewise he who had received two gained two more also.
Matthew 25:17

ACTION STEP

It is now time to figure out how to spend less than what you make so you can have disposable income to save, invest, and give. No one can do it for you. We can inspire you, motivate you, and/or teach you, but you have to handle your own business. Write down your goal of how much you want to set aside for saving, investments, and giving. You may not be able to do it right now, but write your goal and keep it visible. Pray about it, and begin to budget for it. Then go to my website at www.helencrawleyaustin.com/share-your-story/ and share your testimony as you make progress on your goal.

_____

_____

_____

_____

_____

_____

_____

_____

_____

_____

_____

DAY 8

There is a difference between fear and unbelief. Fear, you can cast out. Unbelief, you have to teach it out!
–Pastor Bill Winston

After moving to the western suburbs of Chicago, I attended Living Word Christian Center, where Bill Winston is the pastor, for more than ten years. The biblical knowledge about finances he instilled in me has been invaluable in my personal financial life. I say all the time, "He fed us meat, potatoes, and broccoli!" I never really thought about the difference between fear and unbelief until I heard Pastor Winston speak on the subject. I love people who shed new light on common terms. In my view, that's what separates good teachers from great teachers.

Pastor Winston makes a profound statement in this quote that is backed up by Scripture. First John 4:18 reads, "There is no fear in love; but perfect love casts out fear, because fear involves torment. But he who fears has not been made perfect in love." This Scripture suggests that we can cast out fear by loving who we are and what has been given us to manage regardless of the amount. Unbelief is the absence of faith. According to Romans 10:17, faith comes by hearing the Word of God.

If you don't believe you can and/or should properly manage your money, then I advise you to study what God says about your money. Teach yourself using the Word of God. You can be a good steward of your money!

In the Word...
His lord said to him, "Well done, good and faithful servant; you have been faithful over a few things, I will make you ruler over many things. Enter into the joy of your lord."
Matthew 25:23

ACTION STEP

Read Matthew 28:10-28. This Scripture is a parable about how three people were all given abilities, opportunities, and a designated amount of money to manage. The interesting moral of the story is that an individual created a gain without being told there was an expectation of increasing his designated amount of money. What a teachable story! List the ways you can use your abilities, opportunities, and the amount of money you earn to produce an increase.

DAY 9

You cannot have a rainbow without a storm!
–John Hope Bryant

A rainbow is an optical and meteorological phenomenon caused by both reflection and refraction of light in water droplets, resulting in a spectrum of light appearing in the sky. You can't have a rainbow without the water from a rainstorm. In other words, rainbows are caused by the sunlight after a storm. I have a master of science degree, and I learned that reflection and refraction can cause things that are far away to seem close. Most people have never noticed that the sun is always behind them when they face a rainbow.

Everyone will have some rain in his or her life. Every day will not be sunny, but just know that the sun (Son) is always behind you in your storm. Don't go by what you see; go by what you know. Since you know the rain will come, be prepared for it. Your rain may be in the form of a flat tire. Someone else's rain might be college tuition. The list could go on and on. The question is, do you have an umbrella until your rainbow shines through? In financial terms, do you have an emergency fund? Having an emergency fund is a critical part in obtaining financial stability. You must have a fall-back account to cover your rainy days.

Although it may take you some time to establish an emergency fund, keep your eyes on your rainbow. Your rainbow is your goal. Use the reflection of your goal to give you hope and to bring your goal closer to you. As you move closer and closer to meeting your goal, you will realize that the storm is over and the sunshine is right behind you. Hold on—your sunny days are coming.

In the Word...
And we know that all things work together for good to those who love God, to those who are the called according to His purpose.
Romans 8:28

ACTION STEP

Challenge yourself to have at least $1000 in your emergency fund in the next ninety days. If you already have an emergency fund, challenge yourself to increase it by $1000 in the next ninety days. Write down all the ways you can think of to get this done.

DAY 10

Financial freedom is available to those who learn about it and work for it.
—Robert Kiyosaki

Robert T. Kiyosaki is the author of *Rich Dad, Poor Dad*. I read his series of books directly after leaving graduate school. Although I had just completed my master of science degree in computer science, I still had a parallel desire to build a large real-estate portfolio. So while climbing the corporate ladder, I also bought properties. I worked my job during the day and looked for properties in my spare time. I took notes on his written books and listened to his audio books too. I even purchased his game.

The harder I worked at learning about investing, the more I saved. I knew I could use other people's money, and don't get me wrong, I did. However, I also knew that it would require money of my own. I spent hours reading, researching, and building a team of experts (including an attorney, a lawyer, an accountant, and an investment realtor).

The point is investment properties didn't fall in my lap; nor did I start buying without learning and saving. I encourage you to decide on an investment vehicle to investigate. Maybe it is the stock market, currencies, or even real estate in which you are interested. Whatever the area, diligently research, study, and talk to others who have done what you want to do. It certainly could be worth the effort.

In the Word...
Thus also faith by itself, if it does not have works, is dead.
James 2:17

ACTION STEP

If you had money to invest, what would you invest in? Your answer to that question is the area you should begin to read and research. Determine the area of interest and start by choosing one book on the topic from your local library.

DAY 11

To be a well-balanced person you must be a person in which enthusiasm and self-control are equalized.
–Bishop Tudor Bismark

Bishop Tudor Bismark of New Life Covenant Church in Harare, Zimbabwe, was a guest speaker at a conference in Illinois I regularly attend. Almost every other sentence that came out of his mouth was Twitter-worthy. His ability to connect Bible history to contemporary issues is unmatched.

I have found his statement on equalizing enthusiasm and self-control to be true in my own life. We can't have energy and enthusiasm for life alone and not be well balanced. In my younger days, my goal was to be a millionaire before I turned thirty. I invested in everything—the stock market, oil wells, and was even co-owner of a security company—and went after almost any property within my reach. Needless to say, I lost a good amount of money back then. After realizing that it was not wise to invest in everything that came my way, I began to pace myself and exercise self-control and discipline in my investments. Just because I could afford certain investments didn't mean they were best for me.

I have now learned to enjoy life, play hard, and spend money but exhibit self-control by seeking God before making spending decisions. The bottom line is exhibiting self-control in every aspect of your life, including your money, is critical. When you realize that you are not an owner of anything and realize that you are just a steward or a manager of what you have, life takes on a different meaning. Self-control and reflection become second nature.

In the Word...
See then that you walk circumspectly, not as fools but as wise men.
Ephesians 5:15

ACTION STEP

Be honest: do you have self-control over your spending and saving? Would God be happy with the way you are managing what he entrusted you with? Identify three to five areas in which you need to exhibit more self-control. Then ask God to help you in those areas. Be determined to balance your enthusiasm with self-control.

DAY 12

Don't get stuck on the left side of the colon.
–Evangelist Teresa L. High

I must admit that I was totally confused when I first heard this statement without the full context. After hearing the clever biblical exposition from Evangelist High, I understood that she was using the word "colon" to refer to the punctuation mark, not to a part of the human anatomy. What I realized was she has an innate ability to see in Scripture what few others are able to see.

Check out Luke 5:5: "And Simon answering said unto him, Master, we have toiled all the night, and have taken nothing: nevertheless at thy word I will let down the net." Her point was this: Don't get stuck on the word "nothing." If you pay attention to the words to the right of the colon, you will see that Peter did what God instructed him to do in spite of his past experience.

I want to encourage you to let this be a new day for you. Why have you allowed yourself to experience nothing positive when it comes to your finances? Well, maybe nothing is too strong. Let's just say you have not experienced what you want to experience. You have gone fishing but haven't caught much. Why are you accepting that? You may not have done a great job with your finances to date; nevertheless, by Mastering Money God's way and letting Him help, you will see your increase as Peter saw his.

In the Word...
Simon answered, "Master, we've worked hard all night and haven't caught anything. But because you say so, I will let down the nets." When they had done so, they caught such a large number of fish that their nets began to break.
Luke 5:5-6

ACTION STEP

Go to God and ask Him where to put down your net. What are you good at? What abilities do you have that can bring increase in your life with God's help? Write down one or two area(s) to take to God as possible avenues to bless you financially.

DAY 13

We have to plant and water, but God has the hard part. He increases!
−Pastor Smokie Norful

Most of you know Grammy Award-winning singer Smokie Norful. He's also the pastor of Victory Cathedral Worship Center in Bolingbrook, Illinois, which is my church. In my opinion, he is a prolific communicator both in word and song. His topic of "increase" fits right in with the theme of this book. The message is clear: God has a role to play in our increase, but we have to trust Him while we do our part.

In the message from which this statement is taken, Pastor Norful told the story of Elijah and how God used the raven, a scavenger bird, to usher in his food supply. That right there requires trust. But we also have a role to play. For example, there is a young lady who is a participant in one of my Mastering Money debt-free life groups. She admits that she has not done well in the past with her finances. After making the decision that having her own home and leaving a legacy to her children was a priority, she got to work. She outlined the debt she needed to pay to improve her credit score, started working overtime to generate more income to pay off the debt, and committed to paying all her bills on time. Here's the miraculous part: Her job is giving her as much overtime as she wants, her creditors have agreed for her to repay just a portion of what she owes, and she is on target to purchase her home by the end of the year. This is a great example of her planting and watering, but God giving the increase!

In the Word...
I planted, Apollos watered, but God gave the increase. So then neither he who plants is anything, nor he who waters, but God who gives the increase.
1 Corinthians 3:6

ACTION STEP

God has made many promises to you, but you must do your part. Align with His way when it comes to your finances so you can see increase. What are some areas you need to straighten out to align with God? Have you completed a budget so you can review your spending patterns to have some money left over for future investments? Are you making sure you are not committing to something you can't pay for? Are you paying your bills on time? Are you paying your tithes? Are you giving in both offering and to others? List a couple areas in which you could improve, then pull out the shovel and hose and get to work!

_____

_____

_____

_____

_____

_____

_____

_____

_____

_____

_____

_____

_____

DAY 14

*Stop acting like trials are a surprise to you.
It is a part of the process!*
–Pastor Tim Bailey

Pastor Tim Bailey is the pastor of the south campus of my home church, Victory Cathedral Worship Center in Chicago. He is a humble young man who has submitted to the call of God on his life. I like his approach to teaching because he teaches what he lives. He taught one day in a very down-to-earth way about bad days. His point was that trying to get rid of bad days is not the way to overcome them.

It is in your ability to press your way through them that helps you grow and prepare for the next inevitable test or trial. I could relate to his point. Since life is going to happen, you might as well embrace the ride and learn the lessons God is trying to teach you. The Bible teaches us in 1 Peter 5:7 to cast all our anxiety on Him because He cares for us. The best way to get through your financial trials is to cast them on the only one who not only can provide you the best support but also care for you in the process.

I remember a time while in graduate school when I was dead broke. I was so broke that a newly found friend of mine regularly invited me to her family's house to eat. I remember having to make a decision to buy gas or food by the end of the first semester. The stress of being broke and maintaining my targeted GPA was overwhelming to say the least. The only thing I can attribute to my mental stability was my time in the Word of God. I was studying the Old Testament, which is filled with battles that were won. It kept my faith strong. Although it was a tough situation to gut out, I got through it, and God blessed me with a substantial stipend the following semester because I was able to maintain a 4.0.

In the Word...
And He said to me, "My grace is sufficient for you, for my strength is made perfect in weakness." Therefore most gladly I will rather boast in my infirmities, that the power of Christ may rest upon me.
2 Corinthians 12:9

ACTION STEP

You know how you react to trials. Some people get depressed; others use shopping as an outlet. This results in major regrets months later. I definitely recommend identifying a biblical character that overcame a similar circumstance or challenge from which you can glean. What are other alternative approaches you can take while you cast your care on God during your trials?

_____

_____

_____

_____

_____

_____

_____

_____

_____

_____

_____

_____

_____

_____

DAY 15

You cannot have a harvest without sacrifice.
–Bishop T.D. Jakes

John 12:24 reads, "Very truly I tell you, unless a kernel of wheat falls to the ground and dies, it remains only a single seed. But if it dies, it produces many seeds." Most people only focus on the harvest. However, farmers labor for months tilling the ground, planting and watering the seeds, and pulling the weeds before they reap a harvest. It is a tremendous amount of work to get a harvest.

One day in my quest for learning, I went to visit a farmer along a back country road in Illinois. I wanted to truly understand the concept of seedtime and harvest. The farmer was delighted to share the details of his occupation with me. He talked about the effort required to till the land and the equipment necessary to do so. He explained to me the magnitude of seeds required to be planted in order to get an expected harvest. He showed me the machines used to plant the seeds and water them. I was amazed at the amount of work, time, and sacrifice required for his harvest.

I drove away from the farm excited because, although we don't have the ability to make anything grow, God does. It is guaranteed that nothing will grow if we don't make the sacrifices to till, plant, and water. Being a good steward, or manager, of your money requires sacrifices. We can't have everything we want exactly when we want it. Expect your harvest to come when you are ready to make the sacrifice.

In the Word...
Do not be deceived, God is not mocked; for whatever a man sows, that he will also reap.
Galatians 6:7

ACTION STEP

Are you ready for your harvest? Are you willing to sacrifice a vacation, postpone the purchase of a new car, or forego the new iPhone for a period of time? What sacrifices can you make over the next thirty days?

DAY 16

Believe you can and you're halfway there.
—Theodore Roosevelt

Napoleon Hill's book *Think and Grow Rich* was inspired by a suggestion from Andrew Carnegie. According to Wikipedia, "while the title implies the book deals with how to get rich, the author explained that the philosophy on the power of your thoughts taught in the book can be used to help people succeed in all lines of work and to do or be almost anything they want."[2]

A well-known Scripture, Proverbs 23:7 simply says, "As he thinks in his heart, so is he." There have been many books written, speeches given, and stories told about how important it is to manage your thoughts. How you think and digest the world around you has everything to do with the results you will see manifest in your life.

Take Dave Thomas, the founder of Wendy's, as an example. He never knew his mother and was adopted twice before the age of ten. He dropped out of school in the 10th grade and got a job in a restaurant. How many bad breaks could one person have as a youth? However, Dave did not let the lost of his parents or the lack of education deter him from pursuing his desire to own a restaurant. He couldn't find a good hamburger restaurant in Columbus, Ohio, so he decided to open his own. His successful business all started with a thought that if he could not find a good hamburger restaurant that there might be others who felt the same. What's more critical is, although his childhood circumstances could have dictated otherwise, he didn't let thoughts of inferiority stop him. He believed he could build a successful business and created what has now become the third largest hamburger chain in the United States.

What is it that you think you can do financially? Why not think big? Don't let the fear of failure stop you from thinking about your possibilities!

In the Word...
For as he thinks in his heart, so is he.
Proverbs 23:7

ACTION STEP

What thoughts are you having that may be blocking you from financial peace? Do you think you deserve it? If not, why? Explore your blocking thoughts. Writing them down might help you first identify roadblocks in your life. Then you can develop ways to replace the thoughts with the truth of God's Word.

DAY 17

Look over your shoulder because goodness and mercy is following you.
—Bishop Roy C. Dawkins

Gratitude is a vital component of the formula for a successful financial life. You can't put a dollar sign on gratitude. It doesn't cost anything, but it means everything. You've heard the saying, "Sometimes you have to stop and smell the roses." There are numerous things for which you can be grateful: your life, measure of health, your family, a roof over your head, food on your table, a job, and a car. I could go on and on.

Think about the awesome fact that you have goodness and mercy following you all the days of your life. Wow! When you get bogged down with life, stop thinking about what you don't have and spend time thinking about what you do have. If you can't think of anything else, just look over your shoulders and speak to your two new friends—goodness and mercy.

Goodness is the quality of being good. In the spirit of gratitude, I'm sure everyone can find one financial indication of God's goodness. Think about a time someone gave you an unexpected gift out of the kindness of his or her heart. Sometimes we only celebrate the large financial blessings, but sometimes just pondering over small acts of God's goodness is enough to keep us going.

Mercy is the unmerited favor of God. We've all experienced God's favor in some way or another. For example: have you ever been selected to receive the job, promotion, or contract over someone else? All things equal, then why you? In the process of becoming financially free, let's not forget to be grateful for the small wins along the way.

In the Word...
Surely goodness and mercy shall follow me all the days of my life; and I will dwell in the house of the LORD Forever.
Psalm 23:6

ACTION STEP

Keep a gratitude journal. Sometimes we too easily forget the small financial wins in our lives. With so much bad news in the media, you have to be careful to counter the negative energy permeating our country. Start today! Begin a gratitude journal. As a jumpstart, write down three financial wins you've experienced in the last two years.

DAY 18

Like David, I want to be remembered for being a man after the heart of God.
–Pastor Edward Brinson

Few people make a profound impact on my life upon my meeting them for the first time. Although Pastor Ed, as we call him, pastors a church of over 3000 members, he is still approachable with a personality that is magnetic. Upon being in his presence, you will know immediately that he loves people. Since teaching at his church eight years ago, I have looked to him as my mentor. His quote sums up who he is.

How do you want to be remembered? David's life was infused with many successes and failures; it spotlights the fact that he was far from perfect. What made him a cut above the rest was his heart for God. Even when David got off track, he went to God to request forgiveness and then aligned with His Word.

We have gotten off course with our finances at some point in our lives. I know I have. However, it is never too late to get back on track. The Bible shares a couple ways we can be remembered financially. Here's one: Proverbs 13:22 says, "A good man leaves an inheritance to his children's children." Imagine how you will be remembered by your offspring after you leave earth.

Leaving an inheritance requires us to direct some dollars to an insurance policy, real estate, or savings so that they can be passed down to your next generation.

In the Word...
A good man leaves an inheritance to his children's children, but the wealth of the sinner is stored up for the righteous.
Proverbs 13:22

ACTION STEP

What small step can you take today to transfer wealth to your family? Do you have an insurance policy that covers more than your funeral arrangements? Have you completed a will to minimize and/or eliminate conflicts in the transfer of your material goods? Make a decision to get your house in order. Meet with your attorney to document your will if you haven't.

DAY 19

Your attitude is as important as your action.
—Pastor Leon Forte

Joseph is a great example of having a good attitude in spite of opposition by doing well to those who left him for dead. Joseph is one of the most inspiring men in the Bible who continually maintained a positive attitude while in the middle of adversity. What you think about yourself determines how you act.

Joseph had confidence in his future because of the God-inspired dreams of his youth. As a teenager he confidently shared his destined future with his brothers, which provoked them to hatred. The hatred was so intense that they set out to kill their younger brother. Years later, after being put in charge of all the land of Egypt, he had the opportunity to give food to his brothers due to the famine in their land. Joseph's attitude here displays this point: Giving with the correct attitude is as important as the gift itself.

Giving is a principle that comes with benefits. Giving should come from your heart. When you give from your heart, it is not only about the receiver but also about God. When you confidently keep your heart anchored in God, you will be able to give to those who despitefully use you with the right attitude. Imagine having to feed the same people who tried to kill you. Joseph's story reminds us that you can triumph with the right attitude when you understand your future.

In the Word...
For where your treasure is, there your heart will be also.
Matthew 6:21

ACTION STEP

Are you doing something good with the wrong attitude? Double-check your attitude. Please understand that you have a destiny to keep in mind. It doesn't matter what someone does to you. What matters is how you respond not just on the outside but also in your heart. What are you doing or giving with the wrong attitude? Jot it down and then ask God to help you to have the right attitude. Ask him to help you keep your focus on your future and your destiny.

_____

_____

_____

_____

_____

_____

_____

_____

_____

_____

_____

_____

_____

_____

DAY 20

Trusting God is the least use of your faith.
–Andrew Wommack

I appreciate Andrew Wommack's straightforward approach to ministry. He just lays it out there, like it or not. In his view (and I agree), stewardship is an understanding that God is the source of your gifts, talents, and income. You are just a manager. Manage it well, and He will give you more to manage because you can be trusted. God wants you to prosper and be in good health even as your soul prospers. That's what John prayed for in 3 John 1:2.

John elaborated that trusting God with your money is not for super or mature Christians. This is baby stuff. Jesus taught that trusting Him in the area of finances is the least you can do. If you say you can't afford to give, what you are really saying is I don't trust God. Most people who say, "I can't afford to give" really do have money; they are just spending it on something else. They also are not aggressively eliminating or minimizing their spending so they can give. It is understandable not to give if you are currently struggling, but how long will you remain struggling? How long will you stay being trusted with little? Isn't it time to be trusted with much? I'm ready. Are you?

In the Word...
Whoever can be trusted with very little can also be trusted with much, and whoever is dishonest with very little will also be dishonest with much. So if you have not been trustworthy in handling worldly wealth, who will trust you with true riches? And if you have not been trustworthy with someone else's property, who will give you property of your own?
Luke 16:10-12

ACTION STEP

Get ready for "the much" to come into your life as you get control of the management of your little. Is it not exciting to know your future consists of much more than this? Write out one thing you plan to do better to position yourself for much. How much is "your much"?

_____

_____

_____

_____

_____

_____

_____

_____

_____

_____

_____

_____

_____

_____

_____

DAY 21

Go For It!
–Bishop Howard Tillman

I give credit to Bishop Howard Tillman for being the catalyst in my life that caused me to *go for it!* He was the first person and minister in my life to convince me that the kingdom needed my gift. He saw the administrative and teaching gift in my life before I ever knew it existed.

There were two critical situations in which his guidance was instrumental in the direction of my life. The first was my decision to leave corporate America. I was just like everyone else who says they want out but never does anything but talk. Well, one day the opportunity hit me smack in the face. The corporation I worked for was encouraging more seasoned executives to consider retiring and was offering a handsome package to leave. Although I had climbed the executive ranks to vice president, I was only thirty-seven at the time but still asked if the offer was opened to me. Of course, I received the initial response of "No Way!" However, a couple weeks later, out of the blue, my boss comes back and says, "If you are serious about leaving, I am turning in the packages at the end of the day. You have until then to decide."

The first person I called, outside of my husband of course, was Bishop Tillman. It was the moment I had been waiting for, yet I was scared to death. I had just gotten married, built a new home, and bought new cars and there I was considering leaving a substantial income position. Although he preached a 15-minute sermonette to me that day, the only thing I remember him saying is, "Any decision made out of fear is not of God, because God doesn't give us a spirit of fear." He was right! I had to go against the decision driven by fear. I went for it, and I must say I have made more money outside of corporate America. In addition, my life has been filled with experiences I would have never experienced in a 9-to-5 job.

So remember, when you align your life with purpose and *go for it!* Money will eventually follow.

In the Word...
I can do all things through Christ who strengthens me.

ACTION STEP

If you were headed out on a road trip 1000 miles away, would you not map out the direction before you left home? You might even determine a couple alternative routes. Do the same with your life! Write out the desires of your heart pertaining to your future and take them to God in prayer. This may help you determine a purpose for saving for that future.

DAY 22

Don't get stuck on pause when God wants to release ... FAST FORWARD.
–Valerie Daniels-Carter

I was hypnotized the first time I heard Valerie Daniels-Carter speak. Not only is she a phenomenal preacher, but she is also a prominent businesswoman. She serves on the board of the Green Bay Packers and owns more than one hundred restaurants, including numerous Burger Kings and Pizza Huts. Most recently, she became a minority investor in the Milwaukee Bucks NBA franchise. Her story is incredible, funny, and adventurous. I don't have enough pages to tell it, so I suggest you Google her or purchase her book, *Your Business Is His Business.*

I remember a time when I felt it was time for me to transition into management at my job. I knew deep in my heart once I accepted being ready for the responsibility of coaching and managing others, my career would take off. The challenge, however, was it meant I would have to move from my home state. I was aware that it would open avenues for new and broader experiences, along with substantially more money. Sometimes staying in familiar places doesn't allow one to blossom; for a moment, the familiar paralyzed me. Thank goodness I followed God's direction for my life and moved to Illinois. A new level of opportunity was opened to me. Not only did I get promoted three times in four years, but also my salary more than doubled and I met my husband. Sometimes to get where we are supposed to or need to be financially requires us to move. You may not have to move to another city or state, but maybe to a new place in life.

In the Word...
The glory of this latter temple shall be greater than the former,' says the LORD of hosts. 'And in this place I will give peace,' says the LORD of hosts.
Haggai 2:9

ACTION STEP

If you have a desire to have a successful business either now or in the future, then understand that it requires a significant amount of prayer, wisdom, knowledge, and courage. Is it time for you to make a move? Start reading books about the life of other successful business people. This week, choose a book to read or an article about a person in your position. Most importantly, ask God for directions about your next move.

DAY 23

Don't get caught in the "Pay, spend, pay" cycle.
—Marisa Torrieri

Have you ever had the feeling that all your money goes toward your bills? You work every day to send all your money to your creditors. This is the cycle in which many find themselves. Make a paycheck, spend the paycheck; make more, spend more. To stop the cycle, you will have to determine how to spend less than you make. Sounds simple, right? Well, for many people, cutting expenses is a major obstacle.

I have done personal finance sessions all over the country. One of the exercises included in the session is one where the participants have to determine how to cut costs out of their overextended budgets. It is amazing to see how many people struggle with cutting hypothetical expenses. Imagine the challenge they must have in real life. Unfortunately, the exercise of temporarily reducing some household expenses is a necessary reality for many individuals.

Just recently, we decided to cut our expenses to better align our budget to increase our disposable income. After just a few hours of effort, I was able to reduce our home and car insurance by $700 per year. In addition, I reduced our cable bill by $30 per month. This is something small that few people spend the time to do. I saved over $1000 per year. What a fantastic return on my time! You can do the same. Will you?

In the Word...
In all labor there is profit, but idle chatter leads only to poverty.
Proverbs 14:23

ACTION STEP

I saved $1000 per year in less than two hours; you can too. Are you willing to put in the time and effort required to determine if it is possible to reduce your expenses? What if you can save $2000 per year? You will never know if you don't try. Don't just give your hard-earned money away. Go for it, then save it! Stop the pay, spend, and pay cycle.

DAY 24

Focus on the promise, not the giant.
–Pastor Smokie Norful

Why do we give so much attention to the giants in our lives—even if they are afar off? Our thoughts are many times centered on the financial giants instead of our promises. *What if they destroy me? What if they take my house? What if they take my car? What if they fire me from my job? What if I never get my finances in order? What if I can't stick to a budget? What if I don't save enough for retirement?*

I remember when I first resigned from my corporate job. I left a high six-figure income to pursue real estate investing. Initially, I was excited. I had my goals and plans laid out. I got my real estate licenses in Illinois and Ohio. I took an internship at a mortgage company to learn the industry. I don't know exactly what happened, but after six months, I started focusing on the "what ifs" (giants). Even though I continued to receive my corporate salary for eighteen months, I started thinking about the possible negative outcomes. *Would we really survive financially? Would we hit rock bottom? Would we lose our house and cars? Would we have to move in one of the investment properties?*

I had to go back to what I knew. I started reading the book of Joshua. I will never be able to properly explain the transformation that happened in my mind and in my heart, but the right people started showing up at the right time. The affordable properties began to appear. They were probably there all the time. The point is, I could not see them before. I began to buy like crazy. I had a vision board of my goals and my motivating Scriptures.

I encourage you to keep your mind on your promise of financial freedom. The Scripture says you will lend to many nations and borrow from none.

In the Word...
For the LORD your God will bless you just as He promised you; you shall lend to many nations, but you shall not borrow; you shall reign over many nations, but they shall not reign over you.
Deuteronomy 15:6

ACTION STEP

Sometimes we have "what ifs" (giants) we don't address, that cause us to be anxious. Face your giants by confronting them. What financial "what ifs" keep you up at night? List them out. Now ask God in prayer for the answers to each. Start writing out action possible plans for each. As I did, you will have to take action to eliminate the giants in your life, but take heart: God is with you.

DAY 25

The dream has got to be bigger than your fear.
—Steve Harvey

On Day 24, I shared with you my giants that I hate to admit were fears. They almost immobilized me. I found the thoughts of the "what ifs" becoming uncontrollable. I had many sleepless nights and anxious days worrying about what could potentially happen. Don't get me wrong, you should think about possible outcomes of your decisions and actions, but then quickly take them to God in prayer.

You see, I'm a problem solver by training. However, it became an issue when I could not devise a solution to my own problem. I couldn't figure out how to replace a six-figure income in a specific time frame in my finite brain. I remained in a state of panic until I documented my budget to determine what we actually needed as household income, wrote down the goals I believe God placed in my heart, and spent no more time devising plans about them. I went to God's Word and stayed in prayer for about a month. God continued to remind me of His promises. The dream he gave me began to expand and explode in my heart. My fears were replaced with possibilities. I got my second wind back. Now remember, I was still receiving a salary, so I'm not recommending you do exactly the same. I knew when it was time to move because I was calm. My spirit was no longer anxious.

The fact of the matter is financial challenges have to be managed because they can take you to dark places. There is no better tool I can recommend than the Word of God.

In the Word...
Be anxious for nothing, but in everything by prayer and supplication, with thanksgiving, let your requests be made known to God.
Philippians 4:6

ACTION STEP

What is the financial dream God placed in your heart? I'm not talking about your immediate goal. If you don't have one, ask for one. If you do, revisit it. Find a quiet place where you can spend one hour with God, asking Him to refine, expand, and illuminate the dream within your heart. Don't forget to write down any new thoughts or directions at the end of the hour.

DAY 26

Your faith is only as strong as the tests it survives.
—Dr. Myles Monroe

When I think about the faith to survive a test, I think about Peter in the New Testament. Peter had enough faith in Jesus bidding him to come that he walked on water. If Jesus bid you to do the same, would you drown? Although Peter started sinking, he kept his eyes on Jesus and survived. How many of us get caught up looking at the tests versus keeping our eyes on Jesus? Even when we mess up and are sinking because of our own doing, we can still recover by keeping our eyes on him.

Americans are sinking in debt. You may be one that feels like you are sinking. Hang on, regroup, realign yourself with God and His principles, and save yourself. Peter did not wake up and all of a sudden have the faith to walk on water. He followed Jesus day after day—learning from Him, watching His ways, and digesting His words. Faith comes by hearing the Word of God. No wonder Peter was able to walk on water. If you renew your mind in the Word, you will increase your faith to do what's required to step out of debt. The Bible asserts in Proverbs that we are to lend to many nations and borrow from none. In other words, it is time for you to start positioning yourself to be the lender. It's time to not have to borrow.

In the Word...
So He said, "Come." And when Peter had come down out of the boat,
he walked on the water to go to Jesus.
Matthew 14:29

ACTION STEP

Congratulations, you are a survivor! You have made it through many tests. Believe it or not, your faith grows with each test. Financial tests are not fun, but once you get through them, it is like a load off of your shoulders. Just to remind yourself that you are a survivor, celebrate some of the tests you have passed by writing down a few of them. Then share one or two of them with a friend who will be happy for you.

_____

_____

_____

_____

_____

_____

_____

_____

_____

_____

_____

_____

_____

_____

DAY 27

*There is only debt. And all debt is too expensive—
if you desire freedom.*
–David Bach

Until recently, I bought into the concept of good debt and bad debt. Most of my life, I have operated on the premise that real estate debt was good debt. Don't get me wrong: there are definitely benefits to owning investment properties. It was only when I did the math on the interest did I realize who was making out like a fat cat. Let me give you a hint: it was not I! The banks are making a bundle off the backs of Americans paying mortgages. After my enlightening exercise, the idea of having no mortgage on the real estate looked much more appealing to me. It was appealing enough for me to plan to sell a few to pay off the mortgage of the remaining. Cash purchases may take longer to acquire, but if you really want to maximize your return on a home or investment, it is worth the wait.

I realize everyone is not in the position to pay cash for a home. The point is save for a larger down payment, get a 10-15 year mortgage versus a 30-year one, or just buy a less expensive home for cash and renovate it over time.

It is time for everyone to look at your debt and find ways to invest in yourself and your future by getting rid of it. The average American will pay over $600,000 in interest in his or her lifetime. I plan to be exempt from that statistic! Will you? What could you do with an extra $600,000? Let's get a grip on this epidemic. I declare war on debt!

---

*In the Word...
The rich ruleth over the poor, and the borrower [is] servant to the lender.
Proverbs 22:7, AMP*

ACTION STEP

Define your plan to be debt-free. List all your debts, smallest to largest. Calculate how much you owe. Start with paying off the smallest debt first so you can celebrate accomplishments as quickly as possible. Get mad at debt and be determined to conquer it! Join our Mastering Money movement. Go to www.helencrawleyaustin.com and sign up.

DAY 28

If you don't take good care of your credit, then your credit won't take good care of you.
—Tyler Gregory

Why doesn't everyone have a good credit report since it is just a report and score of both your borrowing and repayment habits? Is it so hard to do what you said you would do? Your credit report is an indication of your borrowing integrity and determines if you are worth the risk to lend. That's why it is good to see what your creditors are saying about you.

According to a Google Consumer Survey conducted by TransUnion, nearly one third (32.7%) of Americans surveyed said they have never checked their credit report or credit score.[3] Creditors report your payment history and amount borrowed each month to one or more of the three credit reporting agencies (Equifax, Experian, TransUnion). Since the information on the report is used to determine the interest rate of the money you borrow if you are approved, paying attention to it is critical to your wallet.

You should aim for your score to be over 700 to be considered a good credit manager. For those who need to repair their credit report, start by committing to paying your bills on time. That is the largest component of your credit report rating or score. Your report is scored based upon the following factors: payment history, amount owed, length of credit history, type of credit, and new credit.

Improving your score can take some time, but I have helped individuals improve their scores by more than 100 points in forty-five days by correcting mistakes and by more than 150 over six months helping them make payments on time. The bottom line is this: if credit management is an indication of your character, ask yourself, what is being said about me?

In the Word...
A good name is to be chosen rather than great riches,
Loving favor rather than silver and gold.
Proverbs 22:1

ACTION STEP

Go to www.annualcreditreport.com and commit to downloading a free copy of your credit report if you haven't done so in the last twelve months. Be sure not only to check your debts for accuracy, but also your name, address, and employers. Don't get discouraged if your score is not where you want it to be. Set a goal for improvement this year. It will happen over time if you commit to taking the action to correct inaccuracies and begin making your payments on time.

DAY 29

Stars can't shine without darkness.
—Unknown

If you have been struggling for years with your finances, I want to encourage you that it will get better with some effort on your part. Sometimes it feels like a dark situation to be sinking in debt, especially if you have a dream and goal in your heart to be financially free. You are not alone. Let's look at a few alarming figures:

- 76% of American families say they live paycheck to paycheck.
- One-third of adults, or more than 77 million Americans, do not pay all their bills on time.
- Nearly 40% do not have any non-retirement savings.
- 56% of Americans feel like they are falling behind.
- More than 25% of American families have no savings at all.
- 60% of adults do not keep a budget or track their spending.
- 40% of adults say they would give themselves C's, D's and F's on their grasp of personal finance.
- Students entering college are offered an average of eight credit cards during their first week of school.[4]

Here's what I want you to know: God does not send dark places, but He sure uses them. You may not realize it, but dark places are blessings in the long run. They make little problems seem meaningless. They toughen you up and make you pray harder. You may prefer the good times, but those are not the times that strengthen you. An exclamation point is a question mark straightened out. Let God take your question marks of when, where, and how to straighten out your finances to be your exclamation point of celebration.

Let's revisit again how to get the ball rolling. Start by determining why you want to be financially free! Then write down your goals, outline your budget, pull your credit report, and manage your expenses. Sounds like a big to-do list, but you can get the majority of the planning aspects done in a matter of hours. Managing your income and expenses is the hard part, but if you learn how to spend less than you make, you will be on the road to financial independence before you know it.

In the Word...

But when he saw that the wind was boisterous, he was afraid; and beginning to sink he cried out, saying, "Lord, save me! And immediately Jesus stretched out His hand and caught him, and said to him, "O you of little faith, why did you doubt?

Matthew 14:30-31

ACTION STEP

Sometimes it is hard to see the light at the end of the tunnel when we are in the middle of a dark place. Focus on the lessons and keep on learning until you see light. What are some of the lessons, benefits, and changes that have taken place in your dark place?

_____

_____

_____

_____

_____

_____

_____

_____

_____

_____

_____

_____

_____

DAY 30

But in the midst of my horror are bright spots that remind me that God is still with me and for some reason has orchestrated my challenge for my good.
—Dr. Rex Crawley

My brother, Dr. Rex Crawley, recently died of cancer at age 49. While conducting research for this book, I started rereading his blogs to find the most appropriate quote from his numerous writings to use as the last quote of the book. I picked this one because I hear many hardship stories as I travel around the country with my message of debt-free living. Few come even close to the struggle my brother endured the last few years of his life. However, in the midst of it all, he wrote of the bright spots.

As I read over his blogs for about the fourth time, I'm so proud of the way he handled his life. He was a giver to the end. After his death, we heard many monumental stories of how and what he gave. He gave away pieces of himself that will never be forgotten. He left a legacy of pride and service to others, including (most importantly) to his sons. I could tell you about how he raised and spearheaded the distribution of millions of dollars in scholarships along with his Kappa Alpha Psi fraternity brothers. I could tell you about the hundreds of high school and college students who benefited from the Black Male Leadership Institute he led. I could tell you about how many Ph.D. students he counseled through the program he directed. I could tell you about how many uplifting e-mails he sent that were read at his memorial service. I could tell you how many awards he received in Pittsburgh. I could talk about how many articles were written about him. I could share how determined he was to combat the isolation cancer patients endure. I could dive deep into many details of his amazing life, but I will leave you with one example of his heart.

Our god-sister lost her mother several years ago. For her and her brother (our god-brother), losing their mom as young people was a tough ordeal for both of them. My brother had a sixth sense about other people's pain. Imagining the impact of the sorrow-filled day the year after her death, he decided to send our god-sister a birthday card on her mom's birthday, including a $100 gift for her. Who does that kind of stuff, right? It was not only an unexpected gift, but it reassured her that her mother was not only loved but remembered. What a display of love and concern. The majority of people would write a post on Facebook at most, if they remembered at all. He could have been having a pity party for himself after a chemotherapy treatment, but instead of concentrating on his pain, he focused on someone else's.

So I say to you when things get tough and you want to crawl in the bed and cry, remember your perspective makes the difference. Instead of crying the blues, look for bright spots and know that God is somehow, some way working it out for your good. We are only talking about money and debt here, not life and death. If perhaps you need an example, turn back to this page of the book and read about an amazing man who did not let pain, disease, fear, or money stop him from making his mark on the world.

In the Word...
And we know that in all things God works for the good of those who love him, who have been called according to his purpose.
Romans 8:28, NIV

ACTION STEP

What legacy will you leave this world? How will you be remembered? Remember, life is much more than money. Is there someone you could mentor? Is there a struggling single mother in your church, neighborhood, or family that you can help? Are you leaving an inheritance for your children and your grandchildren? Do you have an insurance policy large enough to transfer wealth to your family? Don't let life just be about you. Do something but don't just sit around and complain. As your last action item, write down what you want your legacy to be. What will people remember about you?

ACKNOWLEDGMENTS

Writing this book has been a magnificent experience. The process to collate all the notes I have been taking over several years in one place has been exhilarating to say the least. I began to realize how blessed I am to be surround by and positioned to encounter such wisdom from inspiring individuals.

However, I must end thanking several of the most incredible individuals. First of all, my husband, I am who I am because he lets me fly. He is my rock and my friend. It is marvelous when you get to marry your best friend. We were friends for two years before even dating. I love him for being stable, trustworthy, and the best dad in the world.

My two older daughters who gave me early training and practice at motherhood and taught me how to truly love. They are both the essence of beauty mixed with intelligence.

My Kayla, she is the best of me. I love this young lady more than I can express on paper. She is brilliant. The world is awaiting her talent. She will make her mark on the world. Watch for her!

My parents, words can't express my gratitude for the sacrifices they made for my siblings and me. They instilled belief and discipline in my very nature, and for that I will be forever grateful. They continue to cheer me on and are my biggest fans in whatever I endeavor to do.

My younger big sister. She is a phenomenal, confident, strikingly beautiful woman! She changes the environment of every room she enters. She changes lives of others by not just her appearance but also her very presence, her wit, and her words. Sensitive but strong best describes who she is. As her older sister, I love her too hard sometimes (almost smoother her!), but I can't help it. Protecting her is what I do.

My inherited sister and my nephews are my soft spots. Loving them is easy. My life would not be the same without their smiling faces. My sister is definitely one of my heroes. She is a living example of a bounce-back spirit. I'm so proud of her endurance, focus, and ability to get it done.

My friends, BFFs, spectacular advisory board, mentors across the globe are all part of my village and circle of wise council. I appreciate their support and advice.

My Chicago mom, Darlene Stokes-Washington, who is my biggest cheerleader and the classiest, most stylish diva in my life.

My intellectual friends, I must acknowledge you for supporting the composition of this book. To Byron White, Ed.D., Dr. Jeanne Porter

King, and Jennifer LuVert, thank you for your input and direct feedback. A special acknowledgement to my god-brother, Dr. Phillip Cunningham, for lending me his brilliant mind, wit, and charm. Most importantly, thank you for being an outstanding editor, writer, and brother. I owe you one!

My God, who I could not live without. I'm grateful that He is mindful of me, and I promise Him to be diligent in accomplishing the purpose He has laid before me.

NOTES

Introduction

1. http://www.nerdwallet.com/blog/credit-card-data/average-credit-card-debt-household/

Day 16

2. http://en.wikipedia.org/wiki/Think_and_Grow_Rich

Day 28

3. http://newsroom.transunion.com/one-third-of-americans-have-never-checked-their-credit-report-reveals-transunion-study

Day 29

4. https://moneyu.com/financial-literacy-facts College students 8 CC
http://www.statisticbrain.com/american-family-financial-statistics/ No savinga at all
http://www.people-press.org/2014/09/04/views-of-job-market-tick-up-no-rise-in-economic-optimism/ Falling behind
http://money.cnn.com/2013/06/24/pf/emergency-savings/ paycheck to paycheck
http://www.ub-t.com/summer-2013-customer-survey/ do not keep a budget
do not pay bills on time
have no non-retirement savings

Made in the USA
Middletown, DE
16 March 2015